FROM THE ROOT TO THE FRUIT
A JOURNEY TO SPIRITUAL WHOLENESS
BISHOP DR. KEVIN J. HOLLINGSWORTH

From The Root To The Fruit: A Journey To Spiritual Wholeness
By Bishop Dr. Kevin J. Hollingsworth

From The Root To The Fruit
Copyright © 2024 by Bishop Dr. Kevin J. Hollingsworth

Requests for information should be addressed to:

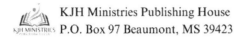 KJH Ministries Publishing House
P.O. Box 97 Beaumont, MS 39423

ISBN: 979-8-9915205-0-8

All scripture quotations unless otherwise noted, are taken from The Holy Bible-King James Version

Cover designed by Professional Style Printing

Printed in the United States of America

First Printing, 2024

Bishop Kevin J. Hollingsworth
P.O. Box 97
Beaumont, MS 39423

kevinrev3@gmail.com@gmail.com

DEDICATION

To the Holy Trinity: Father, Son, and Holy Spirit—thank You for the abundant grace that has carried me through this journey. Your guidance, strength, and presence have seen me through to the completion of this work, and I dedicate every word to Your glory.

To my lovely wife, Shalonda Hollingsworth—your unwavering encouragement and belief in me push me to reach every goal, and your love sustains me. Thank you for always being my greatest supporter and companion on this path.

To my mother, Sandra L. Camper—your constant celebration of every accomplishment fills my heart with joy. Your support has been a source of strength throughout my life, and I am deeply grateful.

To my children, Kristen, Angelo, Ashton, and Aaron—you are my daily motivation. You inspire me to pray fervently and seek the Lord with all my heart. I love each of you more than words can express.

Lastly, to the members of Greater Jerusalem MB Church—thank you for believing in your pastor and for making every moment in ministry a joy. Your faith and support mean the world to me, and I am honored to serve you.

TABLE OF CONTENTS

FOREWORD BY
BISHOP DR. CARRIE JEAN CRAWFORD

It is with great joy and honor that I write this foreword for *From the Root to the Fruit*, a book authored by my dear friend and ministry partner, Bishop Dr. Kevin J. Hollingsworth. Having known Bishop Hollingsworth for many years and served alongside him in ministry, I have witnessed firsthand the depth of his spiritual insight, dedication to the Word of God, and his unwavering commitment to helping others grow in their faith.

Bishop Hollingsworth's passion for uncovering the truth of God's Word has always inspired those around him. In *From the Root to the Fruit*, he masterfully takes readers through a transformative journey, revealing how our spiritual growth is directly connected to the roots we nurture and cultivate in our lives. This book is not just about bearing fruit—it's about understanding the deep spiritual truths that lie beneath the surface, truths that shape and define who we are in Christ.

From the Root to the Fruit is a must-read for anyone who is seeking to grow deeper in their faith and discover the spiritual roots that produce lasting fruit in their lives.

I wholeheartedly support and believe in this work, and I am excited for the impact it will have on the lives of many. Bishop Hollingsworth's message is clear: true transformation begins from the inside out. As you read this book, be prepared to dig deep, challenge yourself, and embrace the change that God wants to bring into your life.

Blessings,
Bishop Dr. Carrie Jean Crawford

INTRODUCTION
THE JOURNEY OF TRANSFORMATION

The journey from root to fruit is one we must all take in our spiritual lives. Jesus said, "By their fruit, you will know them" (Matthew 7:16), indicating that the fruit we bear is evidence of the health of our roots. In this book, we will explore a series of lessons designed to help you identify the root causes of spiritual struggles, remove the barriers that hinder growth, and ultimately bear fruit that glorifies God. Each chapter in this book represents a step in the process of moving from deeply entrenched spiritual issues to a place of spiritual fruitfulness.

CHAPTER 1
FROM THE ROOT TO THE FRUIT

The journey toward spiritual fruitfulness begins with an understanding of the connection between our roots and our fruit. Every tree, every plant, and every living thing that bears fruit does so because it is deeply rooted in something. What we see on the outside is a reflection of what is happening beneath the surface. In our spiritual lives, this concept is no different. If we want to bear fruit that pleases God, we must pay attention to the roots that sustain us.

Planted in the Right Place

Psalm 1:3 paints a vivid picture of a tree planted by streams of water, yielding fruit in its season, with leaves that do not wither. This is not just a poetic image—it is a spiritual principle. The tree's ability to bear fruit is directly tied to its location. It is planted by the water, constantly nourished and refreshed. In the same way, our ability to bear spiritual fruit depends on whether we are rooted in the right place.

"And he shall be like a tree planted by the rivers of water, that bringeth forth his fruit in his season; his leaf also shall not wither; and whatsoever he doeth shall prosper."
— Psalm 1:3 (KJV)

But what does it mean to be "planted in the right place"? For the believer, this means being rooted in Christ, in His Word, and in a community that nurtures growth. It means being surrounded by sources of life-giving nourishment. Just as a tree planted in poor soil or in a dry environment will struggle to survive, so too will a believer who is not grounded in the right spiritual environment. We cannot expect to bear the fruit of the Spirit if we are not consistently drawing from the well of living water, which is Jesus Christ.

"But whosoever drinketh of the water that I shall give him shall never thirst; but the water that I shall give him shall be in him a well of water springing up into everlasting life."
— John 4:14 (KJV)

The location of our roots matters. Many believers struggle because they have planted themselves in places that cannot sustain spiritual growth. This might be a toxic relationship, a job that pulls them away from God, or even a church environment that lacks spiritual depth. We must carefully consider where we are planted and whether the environment is conducive to growth. Are we near the streams of living water, or have we planted ourselves in barren ground?

The Necessity of Staying Planted

It's not enough to simply plant ourselves in the right place; we must stay planted. Too often, we uproot ourselves from the place where God has called us to grow. Perhaps we become impatient, frustrated with the lack of immediate results, or distracted by the cares of this world. Whatever the reason, moving from place to place spiritually can stunt our growth. Like a tree that is constantly being uprooted and transplanted, we become weak and vulnerable when we don't allow our roots to go deep.

"Blessed is the man that trusteth in the Lord, and whose hope the Lord is. For he shall be as a tree planted by the waters, and that spreadeth out her roots by the river, and shall not see when heat cometh, but her leaf shall be green; and shall not be careful in the year of drought, neither shall cease from yielding fruit."
— Jeremiah 17:7-8 (KJV)

The key to fruitfulness is staying planted in trust and confidence in God. When our roots are deep in Him, we will not fear the challenges that come our way. Whether it is the heat of trial or the drought of discouragement, we will continue to bear fruit because we are sustained by God Himself. But the moment we uproot ourselves—whether through doubt, sin, or rebellion—we cut off our source of nourishment.

Roots and Identity

Another aspect of being properly planted is recognizing that our roots shape our identity. A tree is identified by its fruit. Jesus said,

"You will know them by their fruits. Do men gather grapes from thornbushes or figs from thistles?" (Matthew 7:16).

The fruit that we bear is a reflection of our identity as believers. If we are rooted in Christ, we will bear the fruit of the Spirit which manifests—love, joy, peace, patience, kindness, goodness, faithfulness, gentleness, and self-control.

"But the fruit of the Spirit is love, joy, peace, longsuffering, gentleness, goodness, faith, meekness, temperance: against such there is no law."
— Galatians 5:22-23 (KJV)

However, if our roots are in the things of the flesh—selfishness, pride, anger, lust—then the fruit we bear will reflect that as well.

"For if ye live after the flesh, ye shall die: but if ye through the Spirit do mortify the deeds of the body, ye shall live."
— Romans 8:13 (KJV)

Our spiritual fruit is not just something we produce by sheer willpower; it is a natural outgrowth of where we are rooted. Just as an apple tree naturally produces apples and a grapevine produces grapes, a believer who is rooted in Christ will naturally produce Christ-like fruit. It is not something we force, but something that comes as a result of being connected to the source of life.

The Process of Fruit-bearing

Bearing fruit is a process. It doesn't happen overnight, and it often requires time, patience, and perseverance. A tree doesn't bear fruit the moment it is planted. It must go through seasons of growth—seasons of being watered, pruned, and cared for. In the same way, we must understand that spiritual fruit is the result of a process that takes time.

"I am the true vine, and my Father is the husbandman. Every branch in me that beareth not fruit he taketh away: and every branch that beareth fruit, he purgeth it, that it may bring forth more fruit."
— John 15:1-2 (KJV)

Pruning is part of the process. It is painful at times, but it is necessary for growth. The areas of our lives that are not producing fruit must be cut away so that we can focus our energy on what will bear fruit. This might mean letting go of certain habits, relationships, or mindsets that are holding us back. It might mean enduring trials and difficulties that are designed to strengthen our faith and character.

Fruit-bearing also requires a season of maturation. Just as fruit takes time to ripen, so too do the spiritual fruits in our lives. We must be willing to go through the necessary seasons of growth without becoming impatient or frustrated. Too often, we want immediate results, but God works according to His own timetable. The fruit that He is producing in us is meant to last, not to be a temporary show.

The Dangers of Uprooting

One of the greatest dangers to our spiritual growth is the temptation to uproot ourselves during difficult seasons. When we face trials or challenges, it's easy to become discouraged and abandon the place where God has planted us. But this is precisely when we need to stay rooted the most.

"But he that received the seed into stony places, the same is he that heareth the word, and anon with joy receiveth it; Yet hath he not root in himself, but dureth for a while: for when tribulation or persecution ariseth because of the word, by and by he is offended."
— Matthew 13:20-21 (KJV)

When we fail to develop deep roots in Christ, we are vulnerable to being scorched by the heat of adversity. The challenges of life—whether they be financial, relational, or spiritual—will come, but those who are deeply rooted in Christ will not wither. This chapter emphasizes the importance of staying planted and

14

allowing our roots to grow deep so that we can withstand the inevitable difficulties of life.

Reflection and Application

As we conclude this first chapter, take a moment to reflect on where you are planted. Are you rooted in Christ, drawing from His Word and His presence? Or have you planted yourself in environments that are not conducive to spiritual growth? Perhaps you have been uprooting yourself in frustration, moving from place to place, hoping to find the perfect soil without allowing your roots to go deep in any one place.

Take time to evaluate your spiritual environment. Are you near the streams of living water, or are you in a dry and barren land? Commit yourself to staying planted where God has placed you, trusting that in due season, you will bear fruit.

CHAPTER 2

THE YOKE OF BONDAGE

Even after being planted in the right place, many of us still struggle to produce spiritual fruit because we move in and out of alignment with God's purpose. This back-and-forth journey, often caused by legalism, personal entanglements, or spiritual strongholds, can prevent us from remaining rooted where God has placed us. Instead of allowing our roots to grow deep, we become entangled in what the Bible calls the "yoke of bondage."

Freedom in Christ vs. Bondage

Galatians 5:1 gives us a powerful exhortation about our freedom in Christ and the dangers of returning to a life of bondage. The Apostle Paul urges us to stand firm in the liberty Christ has given us and to avoid falling back into the yoke of slavery.

"Stand fast therefore in the liberty wherewith Christ hath made us free, and be not entangled again with the yoke of bondage."
— Galatians 5:1 (KJV)

Freedom in Christ is a gift that was purchased at a great cost. Through His death and resurrection, Jesus liberated us from the power of sin, death, and the law.

Yet, many believers live as though they are still enslaved. Instead of walking in the freedom Christ has provided, they place themselves back under the burdens of legalism, guilt, and fear. This happens when we try to live out our faith by following rules rather than living in the Spirit.

A yoke is a symbol of control. In the context of ancient agriculture, a yoke was placed on oxen to bind them together and direct their movement. When Paul speaks of the "yoke of bondage," he is warning against anything that restricts our freedom in Christ. Whether it be legalism, sin, or unhealthy patterns of thinking, these things keep us from experiencing the full liberty that God intends for us.

The Danger of Legalism

One of the most common forms of spiritual bondage is legalism—the belief that we can earn God's favor by following rules and regulations. While obedience to God is important, legalism places the emphasis on human effort rather than God's grace. It creates a performance-based relationship with God, where we measure our worth by how well we follow certain standards. This mindset can quickly become a yoke of bondage that stifles our spiritual growth.

Jesus spoke against the legalistic mindset of the Pharisees in Matthew 23:4. They placed heavy burdens on the people, making it impossible for them to live in the freedom of God's grace.

"For they bind heavy burdens and grievous to be borne, and lay them on men's shoulders; but they themselves will not move them with one of their fingers."
— Matthew 23:4 (KJV)

Legalism turns our faith into a set of rules to be followed rather than a relationship to be cultivated. It leads to spiritual exhaustion, as we try to earn God's approval through our own works. But the truth of the gospel is that Christ has already done the work for us. We are saved by grace through faith, not by our own efforts (Ephesians 2:8-9).

"God saved you by his grace when you believed. And you can't take credit for this; it is a gift from God.

Eph 2:9 Salvation is not a reward for the good things we have done, so none of us can boast about it."
— Eph 2:8-9 (NLT)

Entanglements that Hold Us Back

Beyond legalism, there are many other entanglements that can keep us from bearing fruit. The Bible warns us against becoming entangled in the things of this world— whether it be sin, fear, or even good things that distract us from God's purpose. Hebrews 12:1 encourages us to lay aside every weight that hinders our spiritual race.

"Wherefore seeing we also are compassed about with so great a cloud of witnesses, let us lay aside every weight, and the sin which doth so easily beset us, and let us run with patience the race that is set before us."
— Hebrews 12:1 (KJV)

These weights can take many forms. For some, it may be an addiction or a habit that they can't seem to break. For others, it may be fear, worry, or anxiety that paralyzes them from moving forward in their spiritual walk. Even relationships or career ambitions can become entanglements if they take precedence over our relationship with God. These are the things that hold us back from walking in the fullness of the freedom Christ offers.

When we allow ourselves to be entangled by the cares of this world, we are like a runner trying to compete while carrying heavy weights. We may still be in the race, but we are not running with the freedom and ease that God intended. I encourage you to identify the entanglements in their life and take the necessary steps to remove them so that you can run your spiritual race unencumbered.

The Importance of Spiritual Liberty

The Bible makes it clear that Christ has called us to live in freedom, not bondage. In 2 Corinthians 3:17, Paul declares that where the Spirit of the Lord is, there is liberty. This freedom is not just the absence of external restrictions but an internal liberty that comes from knowing we are free in Christ.

"Now the Lord is that Spirit: and where the Spirit of the Lord is, there is liberty."
— 2 Corinthians 3:17 (KJV)

Living in spiritual liberty means being free from the guilt of past sins, the fear of future judgment, and the pressure to conform to legalistic standards. It means walking in the confidence that we are fully accepted by God because of what Christ has done, not because of what we have done. This freedom empowers us to live boldly, to take risks in faith, and to serve God with joy.

However, freedom in Christ is not a license to do whatever we want. Paul reminds us in Galatians 5:13 that we are not to use our liberty as an excuse to indulge in sinful desires but rather to serve one another in love.

"For, brethren, ye have been called unto liberty; only use not liberty for an occasion to the flesh, but by love serve one another."
— Galatians 5:13 (KJV)

True freedom leads to service, not selfishness. When we are truly free in Christ, we are free to love others, to forgive, and to serve without the burden of legalism or fear. I challenge you to embrace the full liberty of the Spirit and to use that freedom to bless others.

Breaking Free from the Yoke

Breaking free from the yoke of bondage begins with a choice. It requires recognizing the areas of our life where we have allowed ourselves to be yoked to things that are not of God. Whether it's legalism, fear, sin, or worldly entanglements, we must make a conscious decision to cast off these burdens and walk in the freedom Christ has provided.

Jesus invites us to exchange the heavy yoke of the world for His yoke, which is light and easy to bear. In Matthew 11:28-30, He offers us rest from the burdens that weigh us down.

"Come unto me, all ye that labour and are heavy laden, and I will give you rest. Take my yoke upon you, and learn of me; for I am meek and lowly in heart: and ye shall find rest unto your souls. For my yoke is easy, and my burden is light."
— Matthew 11:28-30 (KJV)

The yoke of Christ is not burdensome. It is a yoke of freedom, rest, and peace. When we submit to His leadership and follow His ways, we find that we are no longer weighed down by the pressures of legalism, fear, or sin. Instead, we are free to live in the fullness of the life He has called us to.

21

Reflection and Application

As you reflect on this chapter, take a moment to evaluate your own life. Are you carrying a yoke of bondage—whether it be legalism, sin, or fear? Have you allowed yourself to become entangled in things that are holding you back from walking in the freedom Christ has provided?

Take some time to identify the specific weights and entanglements in your life. Write them down, pray about them, and ask God to help you release them. Remember, you have been called to freedom in Christ. Don't let anything hold you back from living in that freedom. Stand firm in the liberty Christ has given you, and refuse to be entangled again with the yoke of bondage.

CHAPTER 3
EVERY FRUIT HAS A ROOT

In this chapter, we delve deeper into the truth that every outward behavior, every action, and every spiritual fruit we bear has a root. Just as a tree's fruit reveals the health and depth of its roots, the fruit of our lives—whether good or bad—is an indication of the condition of our spiritual roots. Identifying these roots is critical if we are to experience lasting transformation and deliverance.

In my journey, the Lord revealed something in my heart that I hadn't fully understood—envy. I had noticed how difficult it was for me to wholeheartedly celebrate a friend who was achieving their goals. While they were going hard after their dreams, I had intentionally stepped back from pursuing mine. At the time, I thought that backing off from my dreams made me a better friend. I believed that by not focusing on my own aspirations, I could be more supportive and present for others.

But over time, I realized that something wasn't right. I couldn't understand why I felt a lack of joy for them, and deep down, I struggled to fully celebrate their successes. Then one day, the Lord spoke to me and revealed that my issue was not with them, but with myself. I had allowed envy to take root because I had forsaken my own dreams. Watching someone else pursue theirs stirred up feelings I didn't recognize.

God showed me that this envy was not only preventing me from celebrating others but was also holding me back from pursuing my own goals. I came to the freeing realization that no one could stop me from achieving my dreams—except me. The root of bitterness had weighed heavily on me, and I thought stepping back was the right thing to do for my relationships. But in reality, I was harming both myself and my ability to be a true, joyful friend.

Once the Lord revealed the root cause of my bitterness, the weight was lifted. I was finally able to move forward, both in celebrating others and in going after the things God had called me to do.

The Root of Our Actions

Proverbs 12:3 teaches us a valuable lesson about the connection between roots and stability: "No one can be established through wickedness, but the righteous cannot be uprooted." This passage illustrates that the foundation of our lives—our roots—determines whether we will stand firm or fall. Wickedness, or sin, may provide temporary satisfaction, but it does not give us a stable foundation. Only righteousness, which comes from being rooted in Christ, gives us the security and strength we need to thrive.

"A man shall not be established by wickedness: but the root of the righteous shall not be moved."
— Proverbs 12:3 (KJV)

Often, we focus on the surface issues—our behaviors, habits, and actions—without realizing that these are only symptoms of deeper spiritual roots. Every fruit, good or bad, comes from something deeper within us. Anger, bitterness, jealousy, and fear all have spiritual roots that must be addressed if we want to change the fruit we are producing.

Jesus emphasized this truth when He spoke about the fruit of a tree in Matthew 7:17-18. A good tree cannot produce bad fruit, and a bad tree cannot produce good fruit. The type of fruit is determined by the condition of the tree—and the tree's condition is determined by its root.

"Even so every good tree bringeth forth good fruit; but a corrupt tree bringeth forth evil fruit. A good tree cannot bring forth evil fruit, neither can a corrupt tree bring forth good fruit."
— Matthew 7:17-18 (KJV)

If we want to change the fruit in our lives, we must begin by examining the roots. Where have we planted ourselves? What are we allowing to take root in our hearts and minds? Just as a tree that is rooted in unhealthy soil will produce poor fruit, so too will a life rooted in sin, unforgiveness, or bitterness produce negative fruit. Identifying the root is the first step toward lasting change.

The Root of Bitterness

One of the most dangerous roots that can grow in a believer's life is the root of bitterness. Hebrews 12:15 warns us about the destructive power of bitterness, describing it as a root that springs up and causes trouble, defiling many. Bitterness is often the result of unresolved hurt, offense, or unforgiveness, and if left unchecked, it can poison our entire spiritual life.

"Looking diligently lest any man fail of the grace of God; lest any root of bitterness springing up trouble you, and thereby many be defiled."
— Hebrews 12:15 (KJV)

Bitterness doesn't just affect the individual; it spreads to those around us. When we allow bitterness to take root, it begins to influence our thoughts, attitudes, and relationships. It distorts our perception of others and often leads to anger, resentment, and division. Just as a root affects the fruit, bitterness affects every aspect of our lives, causing us to bear fruit that is toxic to both ourselves and others.

Dealing with the root of bitterness requires humility and a willingness to forgive. It may also require seeking healing from past wounds that have not been fully addressed. Only when we allow God to dig up the root of bitterness can we begin to produce the fruit of love, joy, and peace that He desires for us.

The Root of Pride

Another common root that hinders spiritual growth is pride. Pride is often subtle, hiding beneath the surface, but it manifests itself in behaviors such as stubbornness, arrogance, and a refusal to submit to God's will. Pride was the root cause of Satan's rebellion against God, and it continues to be a major stumbling block for many believers.

Proverbs 16:18 warns us that pride leads to destruction and a fall. Just as a tree with shallow roots is easily uprooted by a storm, a life rooted in pride will eventually collapse under the weight of its own arrogance.

"Pride goeth before destruction, and an haughty spirit before a fall."
— Proverbs 16:18 (KJV)

Pride prevents us from acknowledging our need for God and keeps us from seeking help or admitting our weaknesses. It convinces us that we can handle life on our own, apart from God's guidance. However, the Bible tells us that God resists the proud but gives grace to the humble (James 4:6). In order to experience God's grace and bear good fruit, we must uproot pride from our hearts and cultivate humility.

The Root of Fear

I'm reminded of a woman of God I knew well. She was incredibly gifted and deeply knowledgeable in the Word of God, and her presence was an asset to any ministry or group she joined. However, she had one major flaw—she was extremely controlling. Anyone who spent time with her or grew close to her quickly noticed and often complained about her need to control everything. It wasn't that she wanted anything ungodly, but she felt compelled to control every aspect of the relationships and ministries she was involved in.

One day, during a gathering where people were sharing personal struggles, she opened up about something from her past. She revealed that she had been assaulted as a child. In that moment, the root of her controlling behavior became clear to me. That experience had left her with a deep fear of losing control. When someone takes control from you in such a traumatic way, it can leave you feeling powerless, and that powerlessness drives you to make decisions— sometimes subconsciously—about never allowing it to happen again.

Her fear of losing control became a lens through which she viewed everything around her. Anytime she felt even slightly threatened, that fear would tell her she had to take control back. It drove her actions, even though it was destroying her relationships and leaving her feeling lonely and rejected.

The sad truth was that if she could only confront the root of her fear, she could destroy the negative fruit it was bearing in her life.

Fear is another root that often produces negative fruit in our lives. When fear takes root, it manifests as anxiety, worry, insecurity, and a lack of trust in God. Fear can paralyze us, keeping us from stepping out in faith and fully trusting in God's plan for our lives. Fear is not just an emotion; it is a spiritual force that can take deep root in our hearts if we allow it.

2 Timothy 1:7 reminds us that fear does not come from God, but rather from the enemy. God has given us a spirit of power, love, and a sound mind.

"For God hath not given us the spirit of fear; but of power, and of love, and of a sound mind."
— 2 Timothy 1:7 (KJV)

Fear often grows from a lack of understanding of God's character or His promises. When we don't fully trust that God is in control or that He will provide for our needs, fear begins to take root. The only way to uproot fear is by deepening our understanding of God's love and faithfulness. 1 John 4:18 tells us that perfect love casts out fear, meaning that when we are rooted in God's love, fear has no place in our lives.

29

"There is no fear in love; but perfect love casteth out fear: because fear hath torment. He that feareth is not made perfect in love."
— 1 John 4:18 (KJV)

Uprooting the Bad and Cultivating the Good

Once we have identified the negative roots in our lives—whether they be bitterness, pride, fear, or something else—we must take intentional steps to uproot them. This process may involve prayer, confession, forgiveness, and seeking accountability from other believers. It may also require a deeper study of God's Word to replace the lies that have taken root with the truth of Scripture.

Jeremiah 1:10 speaks of the dual process of both uprooting and planting: "See, I have this day set thee over the nations and over the kingdoms, to root out, and to pull down, and to destroy, and to throw down, to build, and to plant." Before we can build and plant good fruit, we must first root out the bad.

"See, I have this day set thee over the nations and over the kingdoms, to root out, and to pull down, and to destroy, and to throw down, to build, and to plant."
— Jeremiah 1:10 (KJV)

Just as a gardener pulls up weeds so that the good plants can flourish, we must be diligent about removing the roots of sin and negativity in our lives. But simply removing the bad is not enough. We must also plant the good. Colossians 2:6-7 tells us that we must be rooted in Christ and built up in Him if we are to produce the kind of fruit that pleases God.

"As ye have therefore received Christ Jesus the Lord, so walk ye in him: Rooted and built up in him, and stablished in the faith, as ye have been taught, abounding therein with thanksgiving."
— Colossians 2:6-7 (KJV)

By being rooted in Christ—through prayer, studying His Word, and cultivating a relationship with Him—we ensure that the fruit we bear will be the fruit of the Spirit, not the fruit of the flesh.

Reflection and Application

As we close this chapter, take some time to reflect on the roots in your life. What kind of fruit are you producing, and what does that reveal about the condition of your roots? Are there areas of bitterness, pride, or fear that need to be uprooted? Ask God to show you the roots that need to be dealt with and to help you cultivate roots that are deeply planted in Him.

I challenge you to write down any areas in your life where you sense a need for change. Pray over them, and commit to doing the necessary work to uproot the bad and plant the good. Remember, every fruit has a root. What kind of fruit will your life produce?

CHAPTER 4
STILL ROOTS RUN DEEP

Still **Roots**: *Still roots* are deep-seated patterns, beliefs, or behaviors that have remained *stagnant* over time. Rather than growing, adapting, or producing life, these roots have become fixed and lifeless, often rooted in past trauma, unresolved issues, or negative emotions. They choke out new growth and prevent spiritual and emotional flourishing. Instead of allowing healing and transformation, still roots cling to old, unhealthy ways, hindering progress and producing bad fruit.

Roots, whether good or bad, reach deep into our souls—into the very core of our being, influencing our mind, will, and emotions. Like the hidden parts of a tree's root system, these roots weave so deeply into us that we often mistake the fruit they produce—our behaviors, attitudes, and responses—for our true identity. The danger lies in how tightly we cling to these roots, believing that they define us, when in reality, they are often the result of unseen forces, past experiences, and learned patterns of thought.

The Apostle Paul speaks of this struggle in Romans 7:15-20 when he describes doing the things he doesn't want to do, even when he knows better. This illustrates the deep-rooted nature of sin, patterns of thought, and behaviors that have entangled our minds and emotions. Paul identifies that these roots are so deep within us that they shape our actions, even when our conscious mind desires otherwise.

The roots that run deepest in our souls shape how we think, how we make decisions, and how we feel. These roots are often based on past traumas, misunderstandings, or false beliefs we've accepted over time. For example, someone who has experienced rejection may develop a root of fear or insecurity that drives them to overcompensate in relationships or withdraw entirely. This root can produce the fruit of anger, bitterness, or low self-worth, and the person may hold onto this fruit because they believe it defines who they are.

Why Do We Hold on So Tightly?

We cling to these roots because they have become familiar, and we fear losing control. It's easier to hold onto the bad fruit than to confront the root that is causing it. The enemy knows this and uses it to keep us bound, making us believe that the pain or negative traits are who we are. As Proverbs 23:7 says, "For as he thinketh in his heart, so is he." When the deep roots in our soul shape our thinking, they influence our entire lives. We begin to believe the lie that the fruit—whether it's anger, shame, fear, or insecurity—is our true identity.

However, Jesus came to set us free from this cycle. In John 15:5, He explains that He is the vine and we are the branches. When we remain in Him, He can purge the dead roots that produce bad fruit in our lives. But to receive this freedom, we must be willing to face the roots head-on and allow Him to uproot them. This is not an easy process, and it requires a willingness to let go of what we have believed to be true about ourselves.

Overcoming Still Roots

To overcome these deep roots, we must first acknowledge their existence and the fruit they have produced in our lives. This is a call to humility and self-examination, as we read in James 1:21: "Therefore, get rid of all moral filth and the evil that is so prevalent and humbly accept the word planted in you, which can save you." It is the Word of God that will ultimately transform us, renewing our minds (Romans 12:2) and breaking the chains of false identity.

Steps to Uproot Still Roots:

1. **Identify the Root**: We must ask God to reveal the roots that are producing bad fruit in our lives. Psalm 139:23-24 says, "Search me, God, and know my heart; test me and know my anxious thoughts. See if there is any offensive way in me, and lead me in the way everlasting." It is through prayer and the guidance of the Holy Spirit that

we can begin to see the deep roots that have shaped our thoughts and actions.

2. **Confession and Repentance**: Once we recognize the root, we must confess it to God and repent. 1 John 1:9 promises, "If we confess our sins, he is faithful and just to forgive us our sins and to cleanse us from all unrighteousness." This confession isn't just about sin, but about the root causes of our behavior—whether it's fear, pride, or rejection.

3. **Renew the Mind**: After acknowledging the root, we must begin to renew our minds by aligning our thoughts with God's Word. Romans 12:2 says, "Do not conform to the pattern of this world, but be transformed by the renewing of your mind." This transformation happens as we feed on the truth of God's Word and allow it to replace the lies we've believed.

4. **Cast Down Imaginations**: Paul instructs us in 2 Corinthians 10:5 to "cast down imaginations, and every high thing that exalteth itself against the knowledge of God, and bring into captivity every thought to the obedience of Christ." This means that every time an old pattern of thought (root) tries to reassert itself, we must consciously reject it and replace it with God's truth.

5. **Speak Life**: Proverbs 18:21 reminds us that "death and life are in the power of the tongue." The words we speak over ourselves have the power to either nurture or uproot the deep roots

in our souls. We must learn to declare the promises of God and speak life over our situations, no longer reinforcing the false identity that comes from bad fruit.

6. **Submit to the Gardener**: Ultimately, we must submit to God as the master Gardener, allowing Him to prune away the unhealthy roots and guide us into bearing good fruit. In John 15:2, Jesus says, "Every branch in me that does not bear fruit, He takes away; and every branch that bears fruit, He prunes, that it may bear more fruit."

A New Identity

As we allow God to uproot the deep roots that have taken hold in our souls, we will begin to see the fruit of His Spirit—love, joy, peace, patience, kindness, goodness, faithfulness, gentleness, and self-control (Galatians 5:22-23). This is the fruit that reflects our true identity in Christ. We are no longer bound by the false identity that was shaped by the roots of fear, pride, or rejection.

In Christ, we have the power to uproot every deep-rooted lie and replace it with His truth, allowing us to bear fruit that glorifies Him and leads to freedom.

CHAPTER 5
KNOWING IS HALF THE BATTLE

I was having a conversation with a good friend of mine. She was venting about someone who had offered help that she clearly needed, but instead of being appreciative, she was upset. She kept going on about how she never asked for the help and didn't want it. I gently asked, "Why do you think you feel that way?"

Without missing a beat, she responded, "I don't want to know what the root of it is. I'm just talking about what I'm talking about."

This behavior is what I call **Expression**. Expression is the outward release of what stirs deeply within the soul—our mind, will, and emotions. However, without spiritual alignment, expression often becomes little more than an emotional outburst or the release of misguided thoughts and desires. It is an unfiltered response, driven by the flesh, rather than being grounded in truth.

Confession, on the other hand, transcends expression. The Greek word for confession, **"homologeo"** (ὁμολογέω), means "to say the same thing as" or "to agree." Confession, therefore, is not merely speaking what we feel, but agreeing with and declaring what

God has already said. It is the act of aligning our words with what God has deposited in our spirits, boldly declaring His truth over our lives. We must say what God says in order to walk in His promises and experience true transformation.

As Romans 10:9 reminds us, "If thou shalt confess with thy mouth the Lord Jesus, and shalt believe in thine heart that God hath raised him from the dead, thou shalt be saved." Jesus also warned of the significance of our words: "But I say unto you that every idle word that men shall speak, they shall give account thereof in the day of judgment" (Matthew 12:36). Therefore, we must speak intentionally, recognizing that our confessions carry the power to shape our spiritual reality.

That response struck me deeply. If she allowed herself to look deeper, it would likely reveal personal flaws— things she wasn't ready to face. Accepting the help would mean acknowledging that the person offering it saw what was really going on, saw the struggle she didn't want to admit to. And let's face it, to accept help, we have to first acknowledge that something is wrong. But she, like so many others, seemed content to stay angry. It's easier to be upset than to confront the uncomfortable truth that someone sees your weakness and offers a hand.

You must ask yourself, what's more important: my life getting better or maintaining the false personality or reality? The root of that false front is pride. Until we choose to let go of pride, we can't fully embrace the help we need to grow and heal.

As we progress on this journey from root to fruit, it becomes increasingly clear that knowing the root of our issues is a powerful tool in overcoming them. Many times, the lack of knowledge is what keeps us in bondage. The Bible tells us that knowing the truth sets us free, and discovering the root causes of our struggles is the first step toward victory.

The Power of Knowledge

In John 8:32, Jesus makes a profound statement: "And ye shall know the truth, and the truth shall make you free." The key word in this verse is "know." It's not enough for truth to simply exist; we must know it, understand it, and apply it to our lives for it to have an impact.

"And ye shall know the truth, and the truth shall make you free."
— John 8:32 (KJV)

Knowing the truth about the root of our problems is liberating. Once we identify what is truly causing the bad fruit in our lives, we can begin to address it with the power and authority that comes from Christ. Many believers continue to struggle because they never take the time to dig deep and discover the spiritual roots of their issues. They fight the symptoms without dealing with the cause, and as a result, they never experience lasting victory.

This is why knowing is half the battle. The moment you uncover the root cause of your struggles, you are already on your way to overcoming them. But without this knowledge, you may find yourself fighting an endless cycle of frustration and defeat.

The Danger of Ignorance

Hosea 4:6 paints a sobering picture of the consequences of ignorance: "My people are destroyed for lack of knowledge." The word "destroyed" here is significant—it indicates that ignorance has devastating effects on our spiritual, emotional, and physical well-being. When we don't know the truth, we are vulnerable to deception, manipulation, and defeat.

"My people are destroyed for lack of knowledge: because thou hast rejected knowledge, I will also reject thee, that thou shalt be no priest to me: seeing thou hast forgotten the law of thy God, I will also forget thy children."
— Hosea 4:6 (KJV)

Ignorance keeps us in bondage. When we don't understand the spiritual dynamics behind our struggles, we often make decisions based on emotions, fears, or faulty reasoning. This leads to frustration because we try to solve problems in our own strength rather than relying on the wisdom and knowledge that comes from God. Ignorance can cause us to miss out on God's best for our lives.

The Bible calls us to seek knowledge, wisdom, and understanding. Proverbs 4:7 says, "Wisdom is the principal thing; therefore get wisdom: and with all thy getting get understanding." This verse emphasizes that understanding is key to spiritual growth and victory. Once we understand the root of our problems, we can begin to apply the right solutions.

"Wisdom is the principal thing; therefore get wisdom: and with all thy getting get understanding."
— Proverbs 4:7 (KJV)

Exposing the Enemy's Tactics

One of the reasons knowing is so powerful is that it exposes the enemy's tactics. Satan operates in darkness, using deception and lies to keep us bound. But when we know the truth, his lies lose their power. In 2 Corinthians 2:11, Paul warns the believers to be aware of the enemy's schemes so that Satan would not gain an advantage over them.

"Lest Satan should get an advantage of us: for we are not ignorant of his devices."
— 2 Corinthians 2:11 (KJV)

The enemy's strategy is often to attack the root without us realizing it. He plants seeds of doubt, fear, unforgiveness, and pride deep within us, knowing that if these roots are left undetected, they will produce destructive fruit in our lives. When we are ignorant of his devices, we fall into his traps. But once we expose his tactics, we can stand firm in the knowledge that greater is He who is in us than he who is in the world (1 John 4:4).

"Ye are of God, little children, and have overcome them: because greater is he that is in you, than he that is in the world."
— 1 John 4:4 (KJV)

Knowledge allows us to combat the lies of the enemy with the truth of God's Word. When we know what we are up against, we can use the weapons God has given us—prayer, fasting, the Word of God, and faith—to fight effectively.

Knowing the Root Brings Clarity

Once you know the root of your struggle, everything becomes clearer. You no longer waste time addressing symptoms; instead, you can go directly to the source. When a tree produces bad fruit, it's not enough to pluck off the bad fruit and hope for the best. The bad fruit will continue to grow unless you address the root problem. This same principle applies to our spiritual lives.

Matthew 7:17-19 tells us that a good tree produces good fruit, and a bad tree produces bad fruit. Jesus also makes it clear that the root of a tree determines the quality of the fruit.

"Even so every good tree bringeth forth good fruit; but a corrupt tree bringeth forth evil fruit. A good tree cannot bring forth evil fruit, neither can a corrupt tree bring forth good fruit. Every tree that bringeth not forth good fruit is hewn down, and cast into the fire."
— Matthew 7:17-19 (KJV)

If the fruit in your life is bad—whether it be anger, jealousy, or fear—it's not enough to simply try to change your behavior. You must examine the root. Is there a root of unforgiveness that is causing bitterness to grow? Is there a root of fear that is producing anxiety and worry? When you know the root, you can deal with it directly, and the fruit will naturally change.

Knowing the root brings clarity. You are no longer fighting blindly, hoping for change. Instead, you have a clear understanding of what needs to be addressed, and you can approach the battle with confidence.

God Reveals the Root

As believers, we can take comfort in the fact that God is committed to revealing the roots in our lives. He does not leave us in ignorance or confusion. James 1:5 promises that if we lack wisdom, we can ask God, and He will give it to us generously.

"If any of you lack wisdom, let him ask of God, that giveth to all men liberally, and upbraideth not; and it shall be given him."
— James 1:5 (KJV)

God is not only willing but eager to reveal the hidden things in our hearts that need to be addressed. He desires for us to live in freedom, not bondage, and He will give us the wisdom we need to discover the roots of our struggles. Whether through prayer, the reading of His Word, or wise counsel from other believers, God provides the tools we need to uncover the truth.

Jeremiah 33:3 is a beautiful reminder of God's desire to reveal deep and hidden things to us: "Call unto me, and I will answer thee, and shew thee great and mighty things, which thou knowest not."

"Call unto me, and I will answer thee, and shew thee great and mighty things, which thou knowest not."
— Jeremiah 33:3 (KJV)

When we seek God with a sincere heart, He will guide us into truth. He will expose the roots that need to be dealt with, and He will give us the strength to overcome them.

Knowing Leads to Transformation

Once you know the root, the battle is almost over. This doesn't mean that the process of change will be easy, but it does mean that you are no longer fighting in the dark. Knowing the root allows you to take specific, intentional steps toward transformation.

Romans 12:2 calls us to be transformed by the renewing of our minds: "And be not conformed to this world: but be ye transformed by the renewing of your mind, that ye may prove what is that good, and acceptable, and perfect, will of God."

"And be not conformed to this world: but be ye transformed by the renewing of your mind, that ye may prove what is that good, and acceptable, and perfect, will of God."
— Romans 12:2 (KJV)

Knowing the root helps us to renew our minds with the truth of God's Word. Once we have identified the lie or deception that has taken root, we can replace it with the truth. For example, if fear has been the root, we can renew our minds with scriptures that remind us of God's faithfulness and protection. If pride has been the root, we can meditate on verses that teach humility and dependence on God.

Transformation happens when we consistently apply the truth of God's Word to our lives. The more we know, the more equipped we are to experience lasting change.

Reflection and Application

As you reflect on this chapter, ask yourself the following questions: What areas of my life have I been struggling with? Have I taken the time to discover the root cause of these struggles? Am I fighting symptoms without addressing the source?

Take time in prayer to ask God to reveal the roots in your life that need to be dealt with. Write down any areas where you sense a need for deeper understanding, and commit to seeking God's wisdom and guidance. Remember, knowing is half the battle. Once you know the root, you are well on your way to victory.

CHAPTER 6
GET SOMEWHERE AND SIT DOWN

In a world full of distractions and constant movement, many of us find it difficult to simply be still. Yet, stillness is a spiritual principle that is often overlooked. Throughout the Bible, God calls His people to moments of stillness—times when they are to stop striving, stop fighting, and stop moving long enough to hear His voice. This chapter will explore the power of stillness and the importance of positioning ourselves in a place where we can receive instruction from God. It's time to "get somewhere and sit down."

The Call to Be Still

Psalm 46:10 is one of the most well-known verses about stillness: "Be still, and know that I am God." This verse is not just about physical stillness, but also about spiritual stillness. In a world that values busyness, God calls us to pause and acknowledge His sovereignty. When we are still, we can experience His presence and hear His voice more clearly.

"Be still, and know that I am God: I will be exalted among the heathen, I will be exalted in the earth."
— Psalm 46:10 (KJV)

Being still is a demonstration of trust. It is an act of faith that says, "God, I believe that You are in control, even when I am not." Stillness allows us to step back from our circumstances and give God the room to move. In moments of stillness, we are reminded that we don't have to carry the weight of the world on our shoulders—God is in control.

But stillness is not passive; it is active trust. It's about quieting our souls before the Lord and tuning in to His voice. Too often, we are so busy trying to fix our problems that we forget to listen to the One who has the solutions. This chapter challenges you to "get somewhere and sit down" so that you can hear what God is saying to you.

The Power of Sitting at His Feet

Luke 10:38-42 tells the story of two sisters, Mary and Martha. While Martha was busy with the details of hosting Jesus, Mary chose to sit at His feet and listen to His teaching. Martha became frustrated that Mary wasn't helping with the work, but Jesus commended Mary for choosing the better part.

"But Martha was cumbered about much serving, and came to him, and said, Lord, dost thou not care that my sister hath left me to serve alone? bid her therefore that she help me. And Jesus answered and said unto her, Martha, Martha, thou art careful and troubled about many things: But one thing is needful: and Mary hath chosen that good part, which shall not be taken away from her."
Luke 10:40-42 (KJV)

Mary understood something that many of us miss: there is power in sitting at the feet of Jesus. In a culture that values productivity and busyness, it's easy to fall into the "Martha" mindset—thinking that we must always be doing something. But Jesus reminds us that sitting at His feet, listening to His voice, and receiving His wisdom is far more valuable than anything we could accomplish on our own.

This doesn't mean that work isn't important. It means that the work flows out of our time spent with Jesus. When we sit at His feet, we receive the strength, wisdom, and direction needed to handle the tasks before us. But if we neglect that time of stillness, we can easily become overwhelmed, distracted, and burnt out.

The lesson here is simple: don't be afraid to stop and sit at His feet. Get somewhere and sit down, like Mary, and choose the better part. This is where you will find the peace and clarity you need to move forward in your spiritual journey.

Hearing God's Voice in the Quiet

Stillness is essential if we want to hear God's voice. Elijah's story in 1 Kings 19 is a powerful example of how God often speaks in the quiet. After fleeing from Jezebel, Elijah found himself in a cave, feeling discouraged and defeated. He was expecting to hear from God in dramatic ways—through a wind, an earthquake, or a fire—but God's voice came in a gentle whisper.

"And after the earthquake a fire; but the Lord was not in the fire: and after the fire a still small voice."
— 1 Kings 19:12 (KJV)

The lesson here is profound: God's voice is often heard in the quiet places. We expect God to speak through big, dramatic events, but He often chooses to whisper to us in the stillness. But if we are too busy or too distracted, we will miss it. Elijah had to be still in order to hear the gentle whisper of God's voice.

Are you creating space for stillness in your life? Are you positioning yourself to hear the still, small voice of God? It's time to stop expecting God to shout over the noise of your life and instead, get somewhere and sit down in quiet surrender. In the silence, God reveals His heart, His plans, and His direction for us.

Stop Striving and Start Trusting

One of the greatest challenges to stillness is our tendency to strive. We often feel the need to make things happen in our own strength. But in Exodus 14:13-14, as the Israelites stood at the Red Sea with the Egyptian army pursuing them, Moses gave them a word from God: "Fear ye not, stand still, and see the salvation of the Lord."

"And Moses said unto the people, Fear ye not, stand still, and see the salvation of the Lord, which he will shew to you today: for the Egyptians whom ye have seen today, ye shall see them again no more for ever. The Lord shall fight for you, and ye shall hold your peace."
— Exodus 14:13-14 (KJV)

In this moment, God was calling His people to stop striving and start trusting. He was about to deliver them in a miraculous way, but first, they needed to be still. They needed to stop trying to figure everything out and simply trust that God was going to fight for them. The same is true for us. When we try to fix everything on our own, we end up exhausted and anxious. But when we stand still in faith, we open the door for God to move in ways we could never imagine.

Sometimes, the best thing you can do is stop striving and start trusting. Get somewhere and sit down, and let God fight for you. This doesn't mean we do nothing; it means we take a posture of trust, knowing that God is in control.

The Need for Stillness in Spiritual Warfare

Ephesians 6:10-13 calls us to put on the full armor of God so that we can stand against the devil's schemes. It is interesting that Paul emphasizes the word "stand" multiple times. He doesn't tell us to run, to fight in our own strength, or to panic. Instead, he tells us to stand firm.

"Finally, my brethren, be strong in the Lord, and in the power of his might. Put on the whole armour of God, that ye may be able to stand against the wiles of the devil. For we wrestle not against flesh and blood, but against principalities, against powers, against the rulers of the darkness of this world, against spiritual wickedness in high places. Wherefore take unto you the whole armour of God, that ye may be able to withstand in the evil day, and having done all, to stand."
— Ephesians 6:10-13 (KJV)

In spiritual warfare, one of the most important things we can do is stand. Standing is a posture of stillness and trust. It means that we are not backing down, but we are also not striving in our own strength. We are standing firm in the truth of God's Word, fully equipped with His armor.

This is why stillness is so crucial in spiritual warfare. When we are still before the Lord, we allow Him to strengthen us for the battle. We don't rush ahead of

Him or act out of fear. Instead, we stand firm, fully confident in the power of God to overcome the enemy.

Reflection and Application

As you reflect on this chapter, consider the following questions: Are you too busy to sit at the feet of Jesus? Have you been striving to make things happen in your own strength? Are you positioning yourself to hear God's still, small voice?

Take time to "get somewhere and sit down" before the Lord. Find a quiet place where you can be still, both physically and spiritually. Open your heart to hear what God is saying to you, and resist the temptation to keep striving. Remember, there is power in stillness. In the quiet, God reveals His plans, His peace, and His presence.

CHAPTER 7

FIND IT AND KILL IT

In our journey from root to fruit, we often encounter deep-seated issues that have been hidden from view for years. These issues can drain our spiritual energy, rob us of joy, and keep us from fulfilling God's purpose in our lives. To move forward, we must be willing to confront these roots, find them, and destroy them before they destroy us. This chapter takes inspiration from the narrative in 1 Samuel 30, where David and his men pursued and recovered everything that had been taken from them, illustrating the necessity of identifying and eliminating the root causes of our struggles.

The Story of David's Pursuit

In 1 Samuel 30, we find David and his men returning to Ziklag, only to discover that the Amalekites had raided their city, burned it to the ground, and taken their families captive. David and his men were devastated, weeping until they had no more strength. But David didn't stay in that place of despair. He strengthened himself in the Lord and sought God's guidance on what to do next.

"And David was greatly distressed; for the people spake of stoning him, because the soul of all the people was grieved, every man for his sons and for his

daughters: but David encouraged himself in the Lord his God."
— 1 Samuel 30:6 (KJV)

David asked God, "Shall I pursue this troop? Shall I overtake them?" God responded with a clear command: "Pursue: for thou shalt surely overtake them, and without fail recover all" (1 Samuel 30:8). With this divine assurance, David set out to find the enemy, confront them, and recover everything that had been stolen.

This story provides a powerful blueprint for our own spiritual battles. There are things in our lives—peace, joy, relationships, purpose—that the enemy has stolen. Sometimes, we can feel overwhelmed by the devastation, just as David and his men did. But like David, we must strengthen ourselves in the Lord, seek His guidance, and then act decisively. We must find the root of the problem and destroy it before it destroys us.

Identify the Root Cause

The first step in defeating the enemy is identifying the root cause of the issue. In David's case, he knew exactly who had raided Ziklag—the Amalekites. But in our spiritual lives, the enemy's work is often more subtle. It can take the form of fear, bitterness, unforgiveness, pride, or doubt. These are the roots that give rise to destructive behaviors and patterns in our lives.

Hebrews 12:1 reminds us that we must lay aside every weight and the sin that so easily entangles us. These weights are the roots that hold us back, and if we don't address them, they will continue to produce bad fruit.

"Wherefore seeing we also are compassed about with so great a cloud of witnesses, let us lay aside every weight, and the sin which doth so easily beset us, and let us run with patience the race that is set before us."
— Hebrews 12:1 (KJV)

Take time to examine your life and ask God to reveal the hidden roots that are producing bad fruit. Is there a root of unforgiveness that is causing bitterness to grow? Is there a root of fear that is leading to anxiety and worry? Identifying these roots is essential if we are to address them effectively.

Confront the Enemy Head-On

Once you have identified the root, the next step is to confront it head-on. David didn't wait for the Amalekites to come back to Ziklag; he pursued them. Likewise, we must take the initiative in confronting the spiritual roots that are robbing us of peace and joy. We can't afford to ignore or tolerate these issues any longer.

Ephesians 6:12 reminds us that our battle is not against flesh and blood but against spiritual forces of evil. The enemy we are fighting is not a person, but the spiritual forces behind the root issues in our lives.

"For we wrestle not against flesh and blood, but against principalities, against powers, against the rulers of the darkness of this world, against spiritual wickedness in high places."
— Ephesians 6:12 (KJV)

When confronting the enemy, we must use the weapons God has given us—prayer, fasting, the Word of God, and faith. These are the tools we need to overcome the spiritual forces at work. But confrontation is not enough. Like David, we must follow through and ensure that the enemy is completely defeated.

The Danger of Leaving Roots Untouched

One of the greatest dangers in spiritual warfare is allowing roots to remain untouched. It's not enough to address the symptoms; we must go to the root of the issue. In 1 Samuel 15, God instructed Saul to destroy the Amalekites completely. But Saul disobeyed and spared their king, Agag, and some of the livestock. This disobedience eventually led to Saul's downfall and allowed the Amalekites to continue being a thorn in Israel's side.

"And Samuel said, Hath the Lord as great delight in burnt offerings and sacrifices, as in obeying the voice of the Lord? Behold, to obey is better than sacrifice, and to hearken than the fat of rams."
— 1 Samuel 15:22 (KJV)

In the same way, if we leave spiritual roots untouched, they will continue to cause problems in our lives. We must be thorough in addressing the root causes of our struggles. Whether it's a root of fear, doubt, or pride, we must deal with it completely, or it will come back to haunt us later.

Uproot and Destroy

The Bible often speaks of the need to uproot and destroy anything that is not of God. Jeremiah 1:10 describes the prophet's mission to "root out, and to pull down, and to destroy, and to throw down, to build, and to plant." This is the process we must go through in our own lives—uprooting anything that is contrary to God's will and planting seeds of righteousness in its place.

"See, I have this day set thee over the nations and over the kingdoms, to root out, and to pull down, and to destroy, and to throw down, to build, and to plant."
— Jeremiah 1:10 (KJV)

Once the root is identified, we must uproot it through prayer, repentance, and obedience to God's Word. We cannot allow these roots to remain. Like a gardener pulling up weeds, we must be diligent in removing anything that hinders our spiritual growth. This process may be painful at times, but it is necessary for spiritual health and maturity.

Recover What the Enemy Has Stolen

After David pursued the Amalekites, he not only defeated them, but he also recovered everything they had stolen from him and his men. 1 Samuel 30:18-19 tells us that David "recovered all" and nothing was missing—young or old, sons or daughters, spoil or anything that had been taken.

"And David recovered all that the Amalekites had carried away: and David rescued his two wives. And there was nothing lacking to them, neither small nor great, neither sons nor daughters, neither spoil, nor any thing that they had taken to them: David recovered all."
— 1 Samuel 30:18-19 (KJV)

This is a powerful picture of what God desires to do in our lives. When we confront and destroy the spiritual roots that have been holding us back, God enables us to recover everything the enemy has stolen. Whether it's our peace, our joy, our relationships, or our sense of purpose, God promises restoration when we pursue Him and deal with the root issues.

Joel 2:25 speaks of God's promise to restore the years that the locusts have eaten: "And I will restore to you the years that the locust hath eaten." God's restoration is complete—nothing is missing, nothing is lacking.

"And I will restore to you the years that the locust hath eaten, the cankerworm, and the caterpillar, and the palmerworm, my great army which I sent among you."
— Joel 2:25 (KJV)

Reflection and Application

As you reflect on this chapter, consider the following: What are the roots in your life that need to be confronted? Have you been ignoring or tolerating certain issues, hoping they will go away on their own? What has the enemy stolen from you that needs to be recovered?

Take time to seek God's guidance in identifying the roots that need to be destroyed. Pray for the strength and wisdom to confront these issues head-on, using the spiritual weapons God has given you. And remember, just as David recovered all, God promises restoration when we pursue Him and deal with the roots that have held us back.

CHAPTER 8

THE FIVE "WHYS": UNCOVERING THE ROOTS OF YOUR BEHAVIOR

In life, we often experience struggles, setbacks, and destructive patterns that seem to repeat themselves, leaving us frustrated and wondering why we can't seem to break free. We pray, we make resolutions, we even seek help, but the root of the issue remains buried beneath the surface. To fully address these challenges, we must ask ourselves the right questions and be willing to search deeper. One of the most powerful tools for this is the concept of the Five "WHYs."

The Five "WHYs" is a method that helps us discover the root cause of our actions by repeatedly asking "why." It's a simple yet profound process of self-examination, and when combined with God's Word, it becomes a way to open our hearts to His correction, healing, and deliverance. The goal is not just to change our behavior, but to uncover the underlying beliefs, wounds, or lies that influence us—so we can bring them into the light of God's truth and be set free.

Step One: The First Why—Surface Level

When you ask "why" for the first time, you are typically identifying a surface-level behavior. It's the immediate, instinctive response that doesn't take much thought. This might be something you've explained away or justified for years. For example, someone might ask, "Why do I lose my temper so quickly?" The initial answer might be, "Because things aren't going the way I want. "At this stage, we are acknowledging the action, but not yet understanding its deeper cause. Scripture warns us about the dangers of surface-level reactions. James 1:19-20 teaches, "My dear brothers and sisters, take note of this: Everyone should be quick to listen, slow to speak, and slow to become angry, because human anger does not produce the righteousness that God desires." This passage reminds us that our initial response often leads us away from righteousness, and it requires us to pause and reflect before moving forward.

Step Two: The Second Why—Uncovering Patterns

When we ask "why" a second time, we begin to uncover patterns in our behavior. "Why do I get upset when things don't go my way?" This second question might bring up a deeper issue—perhaps a need for control or perfectionism. It is at this point that we begin to realize that our reactions are not just random; they follow a certain pattern or expectation that has formed over time.

Proverbs 16:9 tells us, "In their hearts humans plan their course, but the Lord establishes their steps." This verse highlights the tension between our desire for control and God's sovereign plan. When we seek to control everything, it often reflects a lack of trust in God's ability to direct our lives.

Step Three: The Third Why—Emotional Triggers

The third why often exposes an emotional trigger or response. "Why do I need to control everything?" The answer might be something like, "Because I'm afraid that if I don't, things will fall apart. "Here, we begin to tap into the emotions that drive our behavior—fear, anxiety, or insecurity. These emotional triggers point to areas of our life where we haven't fully surrendered to God. Philippians 4:6-7 urges us, "Do not be anxious about anything, but in every situation, by prayer and petition, with thanksgiving, present your requests to God. And the peace of God, which transcends all understanding, will guard your hearts and your minds in Christ Jesus." When fear or anxiety surfaces, it's a sign that we need to bring those concerns to God in prayer, trusting Him to guard our hearts.

Step Four: The Fourth Why—Identifying the Root

The fourth why takes us even deeper, often exposing a hidden wound or past experience. "Why do I feel like everything will fall apart if I'm not in control?" The answer may trace back to a significant life event—

perhaps a moment of betrayal or a time when trust was broken. At this stage, we are approaching the root of the issue. These moments from our past, often buried deep in our hearts, shape the way we respond to the world today. Psalm 34:18 reminds us, "The Lord is close to the brokenhearted and saves those who are crushed in spirit." This is the point where God's healing begins to work. He doesn't just want to deal with our behavior; He wants to heal the brokenness that causes it.

Step Five: The Fifth Why—Acknowledging the Core Issue

By the fifth why, we have usually uncovered the core issue—the deepest belief or fear that has shaped our behavior. "Why do I struggle with trusting others?" The answer might be, "Because I've been hurt before, and I don't want to be hurt again. "This final why often brings us face-to-face with the lies or unresolved pain we have carried for years. It is here that the Word of God becomes our greatest weapon. Romans 8:38-39 declares, "For I am convinced that neither death nor life, neither angels nor demons, neither the present nor the future, nor any powers, neither height nor depth, nor anything else in all creation, will be able to separate us from the love of God that is in Christ Jesus our Lord." This truth reveals that no matter what happened in the past, God's love is constant and unchanging. It is here, at the root, that healing can begin.

The Power of Asking Why

The five "WHYs" is not just a self-help technique; it is a God-centered process of self-examination. As we repeatedly ask ourselves "why," we allow the Holy Spirit to reveal the deep things within us—things that we may have ignored or denied for years. This process brings the hidden issues into the light, where God can deal with them and bring freedom. In the context of From the Root to the Fruit, this method is a practical way to identify the bad roots that are producing unhealthy fruit in your life. The more you ask why, the closer you get to the truth—and the closer you get to the truth, the more God can transform you from the inside out.

As Jesus said in John 8:32, "Then you will know the truth, and the truth will set you free."

This freedom comes when we are willing to go deep and confront the roots of our behavior. And with God's Word as our guide, we can experience true healing and transformation.

Challenge: Begin the Journey

As you read this, I challenge you to start asking yourself "why." Don't stop at the first answer—go deeper. Ask why again and again until you reach the root. And when you get there, bring it to God. Allow Him to show you the truth, and trust that He will heal and restore every broken place in your life.

Because the fruit you bear is determined by the roots you plant. If you want good fruit, it's time to dig deep and get to the root.

CHAPTER 9
IT'S TIME TO GO DEEP

As we near the conclusion of our journey from root to fruit, it's essential to recognize that true transformation requires depth. Superficial changes may provide temporary relief, but lasting transformation comes only when we allow God to dig deep into the hidden areas of our lives. In this chapter, we will explore the importance of going deep in our spiritual walk, allowing God to penetrate the innermost parts of our hearts and expose the root causes of the bad fruit we bear. This journey calls for vulnerability, courage, and surrender—because real change happens only when we go deep.

Surface-Level Solutions Won't Work

Many believers spend years addressing the symptoms of their struggles without ever digging deep enough to uncover the true roots. We deal with visible issues—anger, fear, bitterness—but fail to go beneath the surface to address what causes these emotions. As a result, we find ourselves repeatedly battling the same problems without experiencing lasting victory.

Jesus spoke to this issue in Matthew 23:25-26 when He rebuked the Pharisees for their focus on outward appearances while neglecting the internal condition of their hearts. He compared them to cups that were clean on the outside but filthy on the inside.

"Woe unto you, scribes and Pharisees, hypocrites! for ye make clean the outside of the cup and of the platter, but within they are full of extortion and excess. Thou blind Pharisee, cleanse first that which is within the cup and platter, that the outside of them may be clean also."
— Matthew 23:25-26 (KJV)

Like the Pharisees, we can become preoccupied with fixing surface-level issues in our lives, but unless we address the root cause, those issues will continue to resurface. External solutions, though sometimes easier, do not lead to the deep, internal transformation that God desires for us. Only by allowing God to go deep into our hearts can we experience true and lasting change.

God Desires to Go Deep

God is always calling us to go deeper in our relationship with Him. He desires intimate fellowship with us, not a surface-level connection. Going deep with God means opening up the hidden areas of our hearts—the places where we have buried pain, unforgiveness, shame, or fear. Psalm 139:23-24 expresses the heart of someone willing to go deep with God.

"Search me, O God, and know my heart: try me, and know my thoughts: And see if there be any wicked way in me, and lead me in the way everlasting."
— Psalm 139:23-24 (KJV)

When we invite God to search us, we are giving Him permission to go beyond the surface and into the deep recesses of our hearts. Here is where true transformation happens, but it requires courage. Going deep forces us to confront the pain, fears, and sins we've kept hidden for years.

It's tempting to avoid this process, to keep things hidden in the hopes that time will heal them. However, time does not heal wounds that are buried—it allows them to fester. If we don't address what lies beneath, we will continue to produce bad fruit, regardless of how much we attempt to fix the surface-level symptoms.

Good Roots Go Deep, Good Fruit Grows Strong

If we want to produce lasting fruit, we must cultivate deep spiritual roots. Shallow roots cannot sustain healthy growth. In the Parable of the Sower, Jesus described seeds that fell on rocky soil. These seeds sprouted quickly but withered away because they had no depth of soil.

"And some fell upon stony places, where they had not much earth: and forthwith they sprung up, because they had no deepness of earth: And when the sun was up, they were scorched; and because they had no root, they withered away."
— Matthew 13:5-6 (KJV)

This parable serves as a vivid illustration of what happens when our spiritual roots are shallow. Without deep roots in God's Word, His presence, and His truth, our initial growth may look promising, but it will not last. The trials and challenges of life will inevitably scorch us if we lack depth in our relationship with God.

Going deep means allowing God's Word to penetrate our hearts, renewing our minds, and shaping our lives from the inside out. It means spending intentional time in God's presence, meditating on His Word, and being honest with ourselves about the areas in our lives that need change. Deep roots allow us to endure life's challenges and continue bearing fruit even in difficult seasons.

The Importance of Inner Healing

Many of the bad fruits we bear—anger, bitterness, insecurity, fear—are the result of unhealed wounds. These wounds may stem from past trauma, rejection, betrayal, or abuse. Rather than confronting the pain, many of us bury it deep within, hoping that if we ignore it long enough, it will go away. But buried pain doesn't disappear; it grows roots that produce destructive fruit in our lives.

Jesus came to heal the brokenhearted and set the captives free. Isaiah 61:1 speaks of His mission to bring healing to the deep wounds of our hearts.

"The Spirit of the Lord God is upon me; because the Lord hath anointed me to preach good tidings unto the meek; he hath sent me to bind up the brokenhearted, to proclaim liberty to the captives, and the opening of the prison to them that are bound."
— Isaiah 61:1 (KJV)

If we want to produce good fruit, we must allow Jesus to heal the broken places within us. This requires vulnerability and the courage to face pain we've ignored. It's not an easy process, but it is necessary for lasting freedom. When we allow Jesus to touch the wounded areas of our hearts, the bad fruit begins to disappear, and we experience the freedom He promises.

Going Deep Requires Surrender

One of the biggest reasons people resist going deep is because it requires surrender. It means relinquishing control and allowing God to do the work that only He can. Many people are comfortable with surface-level Christianity because it doesn't demand much. But true transformation requires complete surrender—offering every part of ourselves to God, including the areas we've kept hidden.

Romans 12:1 calls us to present ourselves as living sacrifices to God. This call to sacrifice is a call to total surrender—allowing God to have His way in every area of our lives.

"I beseech you therefore, brethren, by the mercies of God, that ye present your bodies a living sacrifice, holy, acceptable unto God, which is your reasonable service."
— Romans 12:1 (KJV)

Surrendering to God means letting go of our pride, fears, and agendas. It requires trusting that God's way is better than ours, even when it's difficult or uncomfortable. Going deep requires this kind of surrender because it forces us to confront the things we've tried to control, avoid, or deny. But the reward for surrender is great—when we yield to God, He brings healing, transformation, and peace.

The Danger of Shallow Roots

Shallow roots are not just an issue of limited growth—they are a risk to our spiritual health and survival. Without deep roots, we are vulnerable to being uprooted by the challenges and trials of life. In Jeremiah 17:7-8, we see the contrast between the person with deep roots and the person with shallow roots.

"Blessed is the man that trusteth in the Lord, and whose hope the Lord is. For he shall be as a tree planted by the waters, and that spreadeth out her roots by the river, and shall not see when heat cometh, but her leaf shall be green; and shall not be careful in the year of drought, neither shall cease from yielding fruit."
— Jeremiah 17:7-8 (KJV)

The person with deep roots can withstand the heat of trials because they are nourished by God's Word and presence. Even in times of drought, they continue to bear fruit. This is the life that God desires for us—a life that remains fruitful no matter the circumstances. But this kind of resilience is only possible when we allow our roots to grow deep.

The Depth of God's Love

As we go deeper with God, we also experience His love in a greater measure. Ephesians 3:17-19 speaks of the vastness of God's love, calling us to be rooted and grounded in it.

"That Christ may dwell in your hearts by faith; that ye, being rooted and grounded in love, may be able to comprehend with all saints what is the breadth, and length, and depth, and height; And to know the love of Christ, which passeth knowledge, that ye might be filled with all the fulness of God."
— Ephesians 3:17-19 (KJV)

When we allow God to go deep in our lives, we discover that His love is deeper than any wound, any failure, or any fear. His love heals us, sustains us, and empowers us to bear good fruit. Going deep is not just about confronting our brokenness—it's about encountering the depth of God's grace and love in the process. The deeper we go with Him, the more we experience the fullness of His love and grace.

Reflection and Application

As you reflect on this chapter, take some time to ask yourself these questions: Are there areas in your life where you've avoided going deep? Have you been content with surface-level solutions, or are you ready to let God dig deeper? Are there wounds or hidden sins that need to be brought into the light for healing?

Invite God into the deep places of your heart. Ask Him to reveal the areas that need healing, repentance, or surrender. Don't be afraid to go deep—this is where true transformation happens. As you go deeper with God, you will experience the fullness of His love, healing, and grace.

CHAPTER 10

BREAKING FREE FROM GUILT AND SHAME

Guilt and shame are more than fleeting emotions; they are powerful, destructive states of mind that can paralyze our spiritual progress. While many people believe that guilt and shame are necessary motivators to bring us closer to God, they are actually obstacles. These mindsets keep us trapped in cycles of self-condemnation and unworthiness, hindering us from coming boldly before the Lord.

Contrary to popular belief, it is not our consciousness of sin that draws us closer to God. In fact, continually focusing on our failures disconnects us from the **source of our strength**—God Himself. Instead, our connection to God is through our **spirit**, which has been made alive in Christ. Guilt and shame gain their strength from the false information we believe about ourselves and our relationship with God.

The good news is that there is a way to break free. In this chapter, we will explore the process of overcoming guilt and shame by renewing our minds, casting down imaginations, and making life-giving confessions over ourselves. We will also provide practical steps to institute this process so that we can live in the freedom God has called us to.

Understanding Guilt and Shame as States of Mind

First, we need to understand the nature of guilt and shame. These are not merely emotions that pass with time; they are states of mind rooted in faulty beliefs about ourselves and our relationship with God. **Guilt** is the feeling of regret or remorse over something we have done, while **shame** goes deeper—shame makes us believe that something is inherently wrong with us.

Guilt says, "I did something bad." Shame says, "I am bad."

When guilt and shame are left unchecked, they become strongholds in our minds, distorting how we see God, ourselves, and others. They cause us to feel unworthy of love, forgiveness, and connection with God. Yet the Bible teaches us that we are **forgiven, redeemed, and justified** through Christ.

Romans 8:1 offers powerful assurance: "There is therefore now no condemnation to them which are in Christ Jesus, who walk not after the flesh, but after the Spirit."
— Romans 8:1 (KJV)

There is no condemnation for those who are in Christ. But guilt and shame try to convince us otherwise, whispering lies that we are too far gone, that our mistakes are too great for God's grace. These thoughts are in direct opposition to God's Word, which promises that through Jesus' sacrifice, we are **washed clean and made righteous**.

Guilt and Shame Gain Power from Beliefs

Guilt and shame draw their strength from the beliefs we hold. If we believe that God's grace is conditional or that we have to earn His forgiveness, guilt and shame will thrive. They will gain power from any belief that contradicts the truth of God's Word.

Proverbs 23:7 states: "For as he thinketh in his heart, so is he."
— Proverbs 23:7 (KJV)

This verse highlights the truth that our beliefs shape our reality. If we believe that we are unforgivable, unworthy, or disconnected from God, those beliefs will become the lens through which we interpret our entire relationship with God. But when we align our thoughts with the truth of God's Word, we break the power of guilt and shame.

What we believe—whether true or false—determines how we respond to failure. If we believe that God's love for us is contingent on our performance, we will retreat into guilt and shame when we fall short. However, if we believe that God's grace is sufficient, we will run to Him for forgiveness and restoration, knowing that His love for us never changes.

Step 1: Acknowledge and Confess Sin Quickly

The first step in breaking free from guilt and shame is to acknowledge our sin and confess it to God. The longer we allow sin to remain unconfessed, the more power guilt and shame gain over our minds. The enemy thrives in secrecy, but confession brings everything into the light where God's grace can work.

1 John 1:9 gives us the assurance of God's forgiveness: "If we confess our sins, he is faithful and just to forgive us our sins, and to cleanse us from all unrighteousness."
— 1 John 1:9 (KJV)

When we sin, our first response should be to come to God with humility and confess our failure. Confession is not about begging God to forgive us—He is already eager to forgive. Instead, confession is an act of aligning ourselves with God's truth, acknowledging where we have fallen short, and receiving His grace.

It's important to remember that **God's forgiveness is immediate**. There is no need for prolonged guilt. Once we confess, God forgives, and we must forgive ourselves as well. Holding onto guilt after receiving forgiveness from God is an act of unbelief. If we believe

God's Word, we will accept His forgiveness and release ourselves from the burden of guilt.

Step 2: Forgive Yourself and Release Shame

One of the most difficult aspects of overcoming guilt and shame is the need to **forgive yourself**. While we may accept God's forgiveness intellectually, many of us struggle to forgive ourselves for our mistakes. This keeps us trapped in shame.

Shame says, "I am not enough." It tells us that we are defined by our failures. But the Bible tells us that we are defined by what **Christ has done** for us, not by what we have done. Ephesians 1:7 reminds us that we have been redeemed through the blood of Christ:

"In whom we have redemption through his blood, the forgiveness of sins, according to the riches of his grace."
— Ephesians 1:7 (KJV)

If God, the Creator of the universe, has declared us forgiven, we must also declare ourselves forgiven. Forgiving yourself is not about excusing sin; it's about aligning your perspective with God's. You are not your failures. You are **redeemed**, and your identity is found in Christ, not in your past mistakes.

Step 3: Cast Down Imagination and False Beliefs

Guilt and shame gain their power from the thoughts we allow to take root in our minds. If we allow lies like "God can't forgive me" or "I'll never be good enough" to dominate our thinking, guilt and shame will flourish. The key to breaking their power is to **cast down these imaginations** and replace them with God's truth.

2 Corinthians 10:5 teaches us to take control of our thoughts: *"Casting down imaginations, and every high thing that exalteth itself against the knowledge of God, and bringing into captivity every thought to the obedience of Christ."*
— 2 Corinthians 10:5 (KJV)

Whenever a thought of guilt or shame arises, examine it in the light of God's Word. Ask yourself: **Does this thought align with what God says about me?** If not, cast it down. Refuse to meditate on thoughts that contradict God's promises. Instead, choose to think on things that are true, honorable, and praiseworthy (Philippians 4:8).

Step 4: Renew the Mind Through God's Word

To overcome guilt and shame, you must go through the process of **renewing your mind**. This involves replacing the lies that guilt and shame feed on with the truth of God's Word. It's not enough to simply reject negative thoughts—you must actively replace them with Scripture that affirms your identity in Christ.

Romans 12:2 emphasizes the importance of mind renewal: *"And be not conformed to this world: but be ye transformed by the renewing of your mind, that ye may prove what is that good, and acceptable, and perfect, will of God."*
— Romans 12:2 (KJV)

Renewing the mind is a daily practice. It requires discipline and consistency, but the reward is freedom from guilt and shame. Start by meditating on scriptures that speak of God's forgiveness, grace, and your new identity in Christ. As you fill your mind with His truth, guilt and shame will lose their grip on you.

Step 5: Make Daily Confessions to Break Guilt and Shame

Another powerful tool for breaking free from guilt and shame is making **positive confessions** based on God's Word. Your words have power, and by speaking truth over yourself, you can dismantle the lies of guilt and shame.

Proverbs 18:21 reminds us of the power of the tongue: "Death and life are in the power of the tongue: and they that love it shall eat the fruit thereof."

— Proverbs 18:21 (KJV)

Make a habit of speaking declarations over your life that reflect God's truth. Here are some examples:

- **"I am forgiven and redeemed through the blood of Jesus. There is no condemnation in Christ."**
- **"I am a new creation in Christ. My past does not define me; His righteousness does."**
- **"I cast down every thought of guilt and shame, and I stand in the freedom Christ has given me."**

By speaking these truths daily, you reinforce the reality of God's grace and weaken the strongholds of guilt and shame in your mind.

Step 6: Rely on God, Not Your Consciousness of Sin

One of the most freeing revelations for a believer is understanding that our connection to God is not based on our **consciousness of sin**, but on our spirit. Many people mistakenly believe that the more aware they are of their sin, the more humble or connected they are to God. This is a lie.

Romans 8:16 reminds us of our spiritual connection to God: *"The Spirit itself beareth witness with our spirit, that we are the children of God."*
— Romans 8:16 (KJV)

Our connection to God is through our **spirit**, not through our awareness of sin. Focusing on our failures keeps us trapped in guilt and shame, but focusing on the **finished work of Christ** frees us to approach God boldly. When we are connected to God by His Spirit, we are able to walk in the freedom and grace that He provides.

Step 7: Return to the Source of Your Strength

Guilt and shame disconnect us from the very One who is the source of our strength—God. When we allow guilt and shame to dominate our thinking, we hesitate to approach God, fearing His judgment. But the Bible teaches us that God is a **loving Father** who desires to restore us, not condemn us.

Hebrews 4:16 invites us to come boldly to God's throne of grace: *"Let us therefore come boldly unto the throne of grace, that we may obtain mercy, and find grace to help in time of need."*
— Hebrews 4:16 (KJV)

Instead of allowing guilt and shame to drive you away from God, run to Him. He is the source of your strength, and He longs to help you in your weakness. When you draw near to Him, He empowers you to overcome guilt, shame, and every other obstacle in your life.

Breaking Free: A Process to Follow

To summarize the steps to breaking free from guilt and shame:

1. **Confess sin quickly**: As soon as you fall short, confess to God, receive His forgiveness, and forgive yourself.
2. **Cast down imaginations**: Take control of your thoughts and reject any belief that contradicts God's Word.
3. **Renew your mind**: Fill your mind with scriptures that affirm your identity in Christ and your forgiveness.
4. **Make daily confessions**: Speak truth over yourself to reinforce God's promises and dismantle guilt and shame.
5. **Understand your spiritual connection to God**: Remember that you are connected to God by your spirit, not by your consciousness of sin.
6. **Rely on God's strength**: Run to God, not away from Him, and allow Him to be your source of strength and grace.

By following these steps, you can break free from the strongholds of guilt and shame and live in the freedom and victory that God has called you to.

CONCLUSION
WALKING IN THE FREEDOM OF TRANSFORMATION

As we bring this journey from root to fruit to a close, it's important to remember that transformation is not a destination; it is a continuous process. Each chapter of this book has sought to illustrate the profound truth that spiritual fruitfulness starts with our roots—what we are deeply connected to, what we believe, and what we allow to shape our identity. Along this journey, we have uncovered the key principles that lead to spiritual maturity, but none of these principles will bear fruit unless we fully engage with them in our daily lives.

In the same way that we've discussed guilt and shame as powerful states of mind that hinder our spiritual growth, we must also recognize that every mental stronghold, every limiting belief, and every root of doubt or fear is a direct assault on the life God intends for us to live. The battle for freedom is fought and won in the **mind**, and it is here that true transformation begins.

The Power of the Process

Throughout this book, we have seen how our journey from the root to the fruit requires intentional action. Transformation doesn't happen by accident or by wishing for change; it happens by daily choices, by conscious decisions to reject what the world says and embrace what God says.

Romans 12:2 has been a foundational scripture in these teachings: *"And be not conformed to this world: but be ye transformed by the renewing of your mind, that ye may prove what is that good, and acceptable, and perfect, will of God."*
— Romans 12:2 (KJV)

This scripture embodies the heart of the process. It's the daily renewing of your mind, the daily rooting out of negative thoughts and behaviors, and the daily cultivation of the principles and truths found in God's Word that lead to lasting fruit. Whether it's breaking free from the strongholds of guilt and shame, or discovering the deep roots of our spiritual issues, everything begins with a decision to embrace the **process** of transformation.

From Knowledge to Action

Knowing is only half the battle, but it is an essential half. Each chapter has provided insight into the spiritual principles that guide our growth, but knowledge without action leads to stagnation. If we merely understand the need for deep roots, forgiveness, or renewal of the mind but do nothing to implement these truths, our spiritual growth will be limited.

God calls us to be doers of the Word, not hearers only (James 1:22). This is where real fruitfulness emerges— not in merely hearing the Word, but in actively applying it. Each day presents opportunities to practice the principles laid out in this book: renewing our minds, forgiving others and ourselves, seizing opportunities, and embracing God's vision for our lives.

The Freedom of Letting Go

One of the greatest lessons in this journey is learning to let go of what no longer serves us. As we have discussed in the chapter on guilt and shame, holding onto our past mistakes, fears, and limiting beliefs only serves to hold us captive. God calls us to walk in **freedom**—freedom from the past, freedom from guilt, and freedom from the lies that have kept us from fully stepping into our purpose.

Galatians 5:1 reminds us of this freedom: *"Stand fast therefore in the liberty wherewith Christ hath made us free, and be not entangled again with the yoke of bondage."*
— Galatians 5:1 (KJV)

Letting go is an act of faith. It is a declaration that we trust God with our past, our present, and our future. It's a conscious choice to stop striving in our own strength and to allow God's grace to work in us and through us. This is where the deepest transformation happens— not in our striving but in our surrender.

A Life of Fruitfulness

The ultimate goal of this journey is to bear fruit—fruit that remains. Jesus said in John 15:16: "Ye have not chosen me, but I have chosen you, and ordained you, that ye should go and bring forth fruit, and that your fruit should remain: that whatsoever ye shall ask of the Father in my name, he may give it you."

— John 15:16 (KJV)

Fruitfulness is not measured by temporary success or fleeting moments of spiritual growth; it is measured by a life that continuously reflects the nature and character of Christ. It is seen in the love, joy, peace, patience, kindness, goodness, faithfulness, gentleness, and self-control that we exhibit in our lives (Galatians 5:22-23). This fruit is a natural byproduct of a life that is deeply rooted in Christ.

But fruitfulness is not just for our benefit; it is for the glory of God and the advancement of His kingdom. When our lives bear fruit, we become a living testimony to the world of God's transforming power. Our fruitfulness becomes a beacon of hope, pointing others to the source of life and redemption.

Stepping Into the Next Season

As you close this book and step into the next season of your life, remember that transformation is a journey, not a one-time event. It's an ongoing process of growth, of digging deeper, of trusting God more fully, and of allowing His Word to shape your thoughts and actions. There will be challenges along the way, but each challenge is an opportunity to deepen your roots, to draw closer to God, and to bear more fruit.

Don't be discouraged if the process seems slow. Every season of growth takes time, and some seasons may feel like they bear little fruit. But remember, even in those moments when it seems like nothing is happening on the surface, God is working beneath the surface, deepening your roots and preparing you for the harvest to come.

Philippians 1:6 provides a promise of hope for this journey: *"Being confident of this very thing, that he which hath begun a good work in you will perform it until the day of Jesus Christ."*
— Philippians 1:6 (KJV)

God is faithful to complete the work He has started in you. He is the Master Gardener, and He knows exactly what you need to grow, to flourish, and to bear lasting fruit. Your job is to stay rooted in Him, to trust the process, and to continue walking in the principles you've learned in this journey.

A Final Word of Encouragement

As you move forward, remember that transformation is not about perfection; it's about **progress**. You will make mistakes along the way. You will fall short at times. But God's grace is more than enough to cover your shortcomings and empower you to keep going. Don't allow guilt or shame to stop you in your tracks. Instead, use every setback as an opportunity to learn, grow, and deepen your relationship with God.

The freedom, peace, and fruitfulness you seek are already available to you in Christ. You are already equipped with everything you need to live a life that brings glory to God and bears fruit for His kingdom. The journey from root to fruit is one of faith, perseverance, and trust in the One who has called you.

So, step boldly into this next season. Trust God with your growth, lean on His grace, and live each day with the confidence that He is working in you and through you to accomplish His good and perfect will. Your life is a seed that God is cultivating, and in due season, you will reap a harvest of righteousness, joy, and lasting fruit.

You are called. You are chosen. You are deeply rooted in Christ. And because of this, your life will bear fruit that remains.

ABOUT THE AUTHOR

Bishop Kevin J. Hollingsworth is an inspiring and dynamic leader whose voice has been divinely called to "resurrect a generation with the breath of life." A native of Hattiesburg, MS, Bishop Hollingsworth was raised in the fear and admonition of the Lord, deeply influenced by his family. He credits his musical gifts to his mother, Ms. Sandra L. Camper, and his keen sense of discipline to his father, Mr. Edward L. Hollingsworth II. He is the devoted husband of Lady Shalonda M. Hollingsworth, and together they are the proud parents of four children: Kristen, Angelo, Ashton, and Aaron.

In May 2000, Bishop Hollingsworth founded and became the pastor of Breath of Life Ministries Full Gospel Baptist Church, formerly Ruach Ministries. Under his visionary leadership, numerous ministries have flourished, impacting lives across diverse communities. In addition to his work at Breath of Life, Bishop Hollingsworth was also called to pastor Greater Jerusalem Baptist Church in Richton, MS. His vision for Greater Jerusalem is to be "an oasis in the desert," offering hope and restoration to a generation in need. His mission is clear: to minister effectively to people from all walks of life, crossing social, economic, and ethnic boundaries.

In June 2011, Bishop Hollingsworth was consecrated as the 2nd Presiding Bishop of Maranatha Word Fellowship International under the esteemed leadership of Bishop Dr. Henry E. Williams. His role in this international ministry further highlights his commitment to spreading the Gospel on a global scale.

Bishop Hollingsworth has pursued theological studies at Gulf Coast Baptist Institute (Hattiesburg, MS), Beacon University (Columbus, GA), and Grace School of Theology (Hattiesburg, MS). In 2007, he was honored with an Honorary Doctor of Divinity degree from Gospel Ministry Outreach Theological Institute in Houston, TX. He holds a Bachelor of Theology in Religious Education and a Master of Theology in Pastoral Ministry from Word of Life Bible College and Word of Life Graduate School of Ministry, respectively.

As an author, Bishop Hollingsworth has penned several impactful books: Let Me Go, The Woman Preacher: Fact or Fiction, Tithing and Offering: God's Five-Dimensional Blessing Plan, 12 Reasons Every Believer Should Speak with Tongues, and Teach Me to Evangelize. His dedication to teaching and spiritual growth extends through his role as the president and CEO of Kevin J. Hollingsworth Ministries, which has produced a wide range of teaching materials, including the powerful series: The Power of Obedience, The Power of the Gospel, Something's Getting Ready to Happen, and A Divine Turnaround. His forthcoming projects continue to reflect his deep commitment to sharing God's word.

Bishop Hollingsworth's influence continues to grow as he passionately reclaims territory for the Kingdom of God through his preaching, teaching, music, and unwavering dedication to service. He remains a transformative force, leaving a lasting impact on everyone his path crosses.